THE NATIONAL TRUST

Investigating Design

By Julie Smart
Illustrated by Jane Cope

Designing a better world

Design has an effect on every aspect of our lives – our homes, our school or work, how we eat, play, travel, dress. Everything you see around you that has been made has been made for a reason and designed by someone. Why and how did they make it? What is it made from? Why docs it look thc way it does? This book will help you answer some of these questions. It concentrates the decorative and practical aspects of design, and on homes, inside and out, from walls and windows to tables and lavatories. So if you have the chance to visit an old or historic house, have fun spotting some of the different designs and see if you can guess why and when they were made.

People have been designing and making things for thousands of years. As our lives have become more complicated so the designs have become more sophisticated. Our most basic need is to survive. The solution for early civilisations was to make simple tools – to help them build shelters and catch food – and weapons. Survival was – and still is – a concern. Poor sanitation and living conditions in the nineteenth century led to epidemics of disease. The solution then lay in the design of proper drainage systems and toilets. Health and safety are important factors in the design process today.

Everything is made in response to a need. Naturally, as our needs change, so do the designs. However, not all needs are a matter of life and death. Many designs make our lives easier and more comfortable. We expect our homes to have toilets not chamber pots, carpets not straw and windows with glass, not holes in the wall. Many designs such as patterns on wallpaper or in flower beds – are purely decorative, and have no practical function.

Some needs stay the same – we need furniture to sit and sleep on and vessels to drink from, but we no longer sleep in huge four-poster beds or drink from animal horns or wooden mugs. Each generation develops its own style to reflect the materials available, the technology to make things and the decorative fashions of the day.

Medieval tools

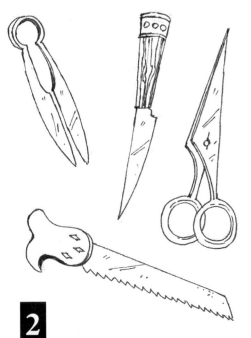

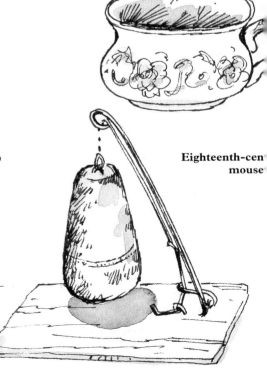

Eighteenth-cen mouse

All materials have different characteristics which make them appropriate for different tasks. A designer must choose the best material for the job. Paper is neither strong nor waterproof, so a paper roof would soon collapse. A chair made of gold might look magnificent but it would be cold, hard – and very expensive!

Some materials are natural, for example, clay, wood, stone. Others have been manufactured or made, such as metal, plastic and concrete. Conservation, or the careful use of natural resources, is a key factor in the choice of materials today as people are more concerned about protecting the environment. For example, bottles were made of glass until plastic was invented. We now know the danger of pollution caused by waste plastic and the trend is moving back towards glass which can be recycled.

Copper hip bath

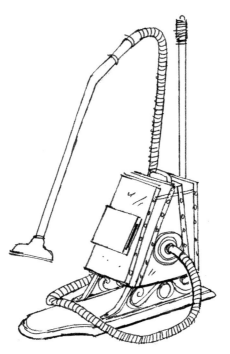

Early twentieth-century floor cleaner

New sources of energy – electricity and gas – have transformed everyday lives and prompted the development of a whole range of household appliances from vacuum cleaners to televisions. We now live in an electronic age where computers enable us to achieve more and more. Computers can even design – though they need people to program them.

When you buy something, how do you decide what to choose? Do you think about the price, how useful it is, how well-made it is, or is it simply how good it looks? Designers have to take all these things into consideration. Appearance – or aesthetics – is very important. You wouldn't buy something you didn't like the look of. Shape, colour and texture all combine to make something look attractive.

Medieval wooden bath tub

In the past, designers made the objects they designed – they were craftspeople. The Industrial Revolution in the late eighteenth century changed all that. It created new and exciting opportunities for designers, but problems, too. Objects had to be designed to be made by machines not people and at first quantity was at the expense of quality. Today, there is a growing demand for handmade goods – 'designer' clothes and furniture – but most things are machine made and mass-produced for reasons of cost.

When a designer finishes a piece of work, he or she must ask an important question. Does it do what they planned it to do? Does it achieve its purpose? It is this process, called evaluation, which means we are continually looking for new ways of using materials, new ways of making things and of improving existing designs in order to make our world a better place in which to live.

Home from home/ Home truths

Our houses today might look different to those built hundreds of years ago, but in many ways they are the same. Whether simple huts or elegant mansions, they are built for the same purpose – to keep us warm, dry and safe. They all have the same basic features – a roof, walls, doors and windows. If these have changed it is because we have different needs or life-styles, because new materials or methods have been developed, or simply because of changing taste or fashions.

Windows are a good example. Medieval castles had small slits for windows because it made them easier to defend – and less draughty! Glass was scarce then and very expensive. Improvements in making glass during the sixteenth century made it cheaper and more widely available. Soon everyone wanted new glazed windows and they became the main features of many houses. Remember that big windows made houses lighter inside and before the days of electric light this was important.

Today many windows are double-glazed to keep out draughts and reduce heating bills. Plastic frames don't have to be painted and are easy to clean. Some people try to improve older homes by replacing the windows with modern designs and conservationists are worried that this changes the character of buildings.

Tattershall Castle

Doing what comes Naturally!

Early houses were not 'designed' as such. They were built by local people from local materials to local designs passed on down the generations. This simple traditional style, known as 'vernacular', was to be copied later by the designers of the Arts and Crafts movement in the late nineteenth century (1831-1915). See page 10/11.

From Sticks and Stones to Bricks and Mortar

Wood is the oldest of building materials. It is light but strong and easy to use. Wood looks attractive and lasts a long time if treated. It can be used to make whole buildings – floors, walls and roofs as well as window frames and doors.

Stone is the most hard-wearing of all building materials but expensive as it is difficult to quarry. It varies in colour and texture, from pale golden Cotswold stone to the grey sandstones of the Pennines. Different stones are suitable for different purposes. The softer limestones, such as Bath stone, lend themselves to ornamental work. Granite is known for its great strength and durability. For many years, the use of stone was a sign of wealth. Most cottages were built of earth or cob, a mixture of straw and wet earth – or even cow dung!

The availability of new materials influenced design. Bricks have been made for thousands of years but were not used much in Britain until the fifteenth century. Tattershall Castle in Lincolnshire, built in the 1430s, is one of the earliest examples of the use of brick, while the gate tower at fifteenth-century Oxburgh Hall in Norfolk shows how bricklaying skills had already developed into a real art.

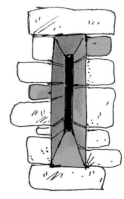

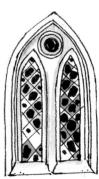

Bricks became even more popular for safety reasons. After the Great Fire of London in 1666, people realised the dangers of wooden buildings and a law was passed making it compulsory to rebuild half-timbered houses in London with brick or stone walls. Bricks were often used in areas where there were no other suitable building materials. Provided there was suitable clay, they were made on site, moulded by hand and baked in special ovens or kilns. After the Industrial Revolution, they were made by machine to a standard size and transported all over the country.

Weather boarding

Wordsearch

Hidden in the wordsearch below are 9 different building materials. Can you find them all? *[Answers on page 32]*

O	N	C	R	E	T	E
A	O	B	H	C	Y	A
T	R	A	W	J	S	R
T	I	V	O	E	S	T
W	O	F	O	L	A	H
G	D	N	D	O	L	I
M	N	Z	E	Q	G	R
B	R	I	C	K	S	U

The Time, The Place

Most buildings reflect the style of the age in which they were built – the Tudors are famous for their half-timbered buildings, the Georgian taste was for elegance and classical proportions. But just as you can tell when a house was built by looking at it, so you can tell where it is. Each region has its own traditional or 'vernacular' style which reflects the building materials available in that area.

Timber framed houses are more common in areas such as Warwickshire and Worcestershire where forests once grew. In the Cotswolds, Yorkshire and Derbyshire local stone is plentiful. Weather boarding is a typical Essex and Sussex style, designed to protect houses against the coastal rain and gales. Many coastal towns have houses made from rough or split flints collected from the beach.

Thatch is perhaps seen at its best in Norfolk where reeds used grow everywhere in the marshes. The most common type of thatch is straw. Thatch is used because it is the lightest of roofing materials. Houses built of unbaked earth or cob, such as in Devon, would simply collapse under the weight of anything else!

Flint

Drawing on Experience

The first step in designing a house is for the designer or architect to find out what the people who are going to live in it want. What kind of house do they need? This is called a design brief.

For example, how many people are going to live there? How many bedrooms do they need? What you can afford also influences the size of the building and the materials from which it can be built.

The next stage in the design process is for the architect to sketch out their ideas. A plan – a view looking down from above – is drawn to show the size and layout of the rooms. Plans are drawn to scale, for example 1 metre of the building is represented by 1cm on the plan.

An elevation, or side view, shows what the house will look like from the outside.

Here is a sketch of how the architect Adam intended part of the dining room at Kedelston Hall to look.

Did the room turn out as he had planned?

Practical developments in design have made our lives easier, more comfortable and even healthier. For example, advances in technology have made it possible for us all to have toilets which flush and taps with hot and cold running water. We have light at the flick of a switch instead of having to light oil lamps or candles. But people spend a lot of time in their homes and they also expect them to look good. Appearance – or aesthetics – is just as important as function if something is to serve its purpose.

Fireside Stories

Fires in early houses were in the middle of rooms and smoke escaped through a hole in the roof. This central hearth was inconvenient and dangerous. The solution was to place the fireplace against the wall, enclose it with brick or stone and connect it to a funnel or a chimney. This innovation was a great improvement. It made houses cleaner, less smoky, and safer. It meant that rooms could be built upstairs.

Today, central heating means that houses don't need open fires and chimneys but many people choose to keep them for the atmosphere they create in a room.

Making an Entrance

Doors are functional – they give access into houses or rooms and thought has to be given to their position. In large Tudor houses, however, doors became features in their own right. They were often made a focal point by placing them within elaborately carved frames or flanked by ornamental columns. Size was crucial as not only did they have to match the proportion of the rooms but they also had to be big enough for ladies with wide skirts and men wearing hats.

Where's the Bathroom?

When you visit an old stately home, do you ever wonder where the bathroom or toilet was? If it's a very old house then there probably wasn't one. For years people even thought it was unhealthy to wash. Victorians would have had a wash-stand in their bedroom or dressing room with a basin of cold water and a jug. Water was heated over the fire.

Toilets were usually outside. Chamber pots were kept under the bed to save a trip to the bottom of the garden during the night! Wealthier households had 'close-stools' – wooden seats with removable containers in a box below which servants had to empty.

Public Health Acts during the 1800s made it law for houses to have proper drains and their own fixed toilets – although outside.

Step by Step

Early houses were single storey – there was no need for stairs. Lack of space in narrow streets and improved knowledge of building techniques meant that many houses grew upwards rather than outwards. Staircases were often spiral because they took up less room and were cheaper to build than a straight one. They were an important part of the design in castles because they were easy to defend; the person coming downstairs (defending) could fight more easily with their sword in their right hand, than the person coming up (attacking).

By Tudor times, defence was less of a problem. Large country houses would have a long gallery upstairs which was used for entertaining and people wanted grander staircases to impress their guests.

Rooms with a View

If you want an impression of the sheer variety of historical interiors all under one roof, then there's no better place to visit than Sutton House in London. There you will find Tudor panelled rooms, an elegant Georgian parlour, a dark Victorian study, and an Edwardian hall – all under one roof! Little panels in the older rooms open like doors to reveal still older layers beneath.

Can you spot the elements that are out of place in this Tudor room?

The Finishing Touches

The Scottish architect, Robert Adam (1728-92), designed everything inside houses as well as outside, down to the last detail – from the furniture, carpets, ceilings and fireplaces to keyholes and doorknobs! Entire rooms were planned as a whole – he even marked the positions for mirrors and pictures on his plan for the walls!

The furniture in some of his rooms, such as the Saloon at Saltram in Devon, was arranged around the wall, so as not to hide the carpet which he designed to echo the pattern on the ceiling.

An Eye for Colour

Painted walls make quite a difference to a room. Certain colours have been fashionable in certain historical eras, for example, neo-Classicists such as Robert Adam preferred pale pastel shades. 'Neo' means new and is used to refer to the revival of an older style. The Victorians were famous for their rich dark reds and greens.

The Tudors

Most ordinary homes in Tudor times (1485-1603) were half timbered – they had wooden frames and the spaces between were filled with small sticks and wet clay called wattle and daub. Glass was expensive so windows were small; small diamond or square panes were set in lead strips and supported by stone uprights or mullions. People who couldn't afford glass used polished horn, cloth or even paper.

The rich in large country mansions which were often designed to a symmetrical plan – E and H shapes were popular. Glass was a fashionable novelty and became a status symbol. Windows became the main features of many houses. Hardwick Hall, the great Elizabethan mansion in Derbyshire with huge windows on all sides, was mocked at the time for being 'more glass than walls'. The great seventeenth-century houses, Sudbury Hall in Derbyshire and Ham House in Surrey, also have fine examples of huge glass windows.

The 1930s

There was a great demand for new houses after World War I (1914-18). New motor cars and better public transport meant that people could live away from their place of work and they were attracted by the new style of house which was being built, especially on the outskirts of towns or suburbs. Many had gardens and some had drives for cars or even garages. Bay windows at the front, upstairs and downstairs, made rooms light and airy. Many semi-detached homes were designed to look like cottages with leaded windows and wood patterns in imitation of half-timbered houses.

The Georgians

A typical Georgian house of the eighteenth century was elegant and formal in style. The Georgians were influenced by the sixteenth-century Italian architect Palladio who had written several important books on classical architecture and many classical features such as pilasters (or ornamental columns) were copied.

In earlier times, 'mullioned' windows had been common. These were windows divided into panels each of which was further divided into panes. Sash windows became fashionable now that it was possible for glass to be made in larger sheets. They opened by pushing half upwards or downwards.

People no longer needed big houses with lots of rooms for servants. Families had less children and more money. They wanted homes to be clean and easy to run and all the new semi-detached houses had electric lighting and electric power points in each room, making it possible to use new labour saving devices such as vacuum cleaners.

The Victorians

During the nineteenth-century more and more people moved into the new industrial towns to work in the mills and factories and rows of terraced back-to-back houses were built to house them. These houses were very small with two rooms upstairs and two downstairs. There were no gardens, only small back yards with outside toilets. Overcrowding and poor sanitation meant that disease spread quickly. Conditions improved after a Public Heath Act in 1875 made it law for houses to have drains.

The development of the railway network meant that building materials could be transported anywhere in the country all looked the same.

Family homes for the new middle classes had to be big enough to house servants and were often ornate with turrets, spires and elaborate details in a style known as 'Gothic'.

Patterns for a purpose

Artists are inspired by beautiful patterns in nature, but people have also learned from nature's example. Many patterns, such as a honeycomb, are made by shapes fitting neatly together in mathematical regularity. This makes them strong, as does the frame structure of a spider's web. Such natural forms have slowly evolved over thousands of years. We can copy these, adapting them to our own needs.

Crenellations

Machicolations

Defensive Details

Houses – or castles – built for fortification had little need for decoration, so any ornamental details you can see are there for a reason. Take the pattern round the top of battlement walls, called crenellations. It was designed so that the defenders could fire weapons through the gaps and shelter behind the solid parts. Another device was machicolations – openings in the floor of an overhanging wall through which missiles could be dropped on the enemy below.

Another Brick in the Wall

If your house or school is built of brick, look at how the bricks have been laid. Do they form a pattern? The interlocking patterns are designed to make the wall strong. See how they are arranged so that weak vertical joints are not one above the other. Stretcher bond is the most common pattern on modern houses with cavity walls – two separate walls with a gap between designed to provide insulation and keep out damp. Flemish and English bonds are used when walls need to be of double thickness for extra strength.

Here are three examples of common patterns or bonds:

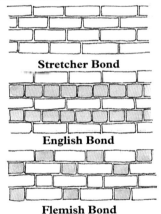

Stretcher Bond

English Bond

Flemish Bond

See the light

In the sixteenth century, people were still experimenting with how to make glass and they simply didn't know how to make it strong enough to use in the huge sheets we have today. Small panes were set in leaded frames to make a lattice pattern.

Glass was still a novelty and some builders took the opportunity to make windows decorative features as well. The glazing patterns of the leaded windows at Little Moreton Hall vary from room to room and even from window to window.

You've been Framed!

The patterned black and white timber walls of many medieval and Tudor homes not only look marvellous but they are also holding the building together! The timbers form a framework which support the building.

Many modern buildings still have structural frames but today they are made from steel or reinforced concrete.

Moreton Crest at Little Moreton Hall

The pattern principle

One of the basic elements of good design is that an object should not only work well and suit the function for which it was made, but it should also look nice. People have to like it. William Morris, the great nineteenth-century designer famous for his wallpapers and textiles, said: 'Have nothing in your house that you do not know to be useful or believe to be beautiful'. The most common decorative features on everything from buildings to biscuit tins are patterns.

Patterns are made by arranging lines, shapes and colours in different ways. Some take one shape and repeat it over and over again in a geometric and quite formal style. Others use natural imagery such as plants with curling leaves and twisting stems. Patterns are designed to fit the objects they decorate so, for example, designs for plates tend to be circular. Like colour, patterns can also be used to create illusions or special effects such as making a room seem bigger or smaller.

Arlington Court

Floor Show

Wealthy Romans enjoyed comfortable and pleasant surroundings. They also ate while reclining on low couches, so it made sense that their floors should be colourful and attractive to look at. They created beautiful patterns on them in small pieces of coloured stone or glass, called mosaic, which was also easy to clean.

Detail of mosaic at Chedworth

Painted floor at Belton House

In the Middle Ages, floors were covered with rushes or straw – no-one would have noticed if there were patterns underneath! But by the seventeenth century, people were taking more of an interest. Marble became fashionable, often in black and white chequerboard patterns, and wooden floors were painted or inlaid with various coloured woods in different patterns known as marquetry. Today we like patterned rugs and carpets to look attractive as well as provide warmth and comfort.

Wallflowers

We have not always had the technology to make patterned wallpaper. Early English wallpaper was hand printed using wooden blocks. It was a slow, laborious process which made the paper expensive. Mechanisation and mass production in the early nineteenth century revolutionised the printing process, making wallpapers cheaper and more accessible, but it was one man who revolutionised the design.

William Morris (1834-1896) is perhaps the most famous and important designer of the Victorian era. His wallpaper and fabric designs are still produced and bought today.

Morris took his inspiration from nature and most of his designs feature flowers, fruit or leaves. They are also two-dimensional, emphasising the flatness of the wall. Because he did not like the commercial dyes available, he experimented with traditional vegetable dyes.

Morris was one of a group of designers who formed what was to become known as the Arts and Crafts Movement. They wanted to encourage the values of craftsmanship and were against the use of machines. The work of the Arts and Crafts Movement was highly decorative, inspired by an interest in the art and design of the Middle Ages.

Standen, in West Sussex, is full of Morris wallpapers, furnishing fabrics and furniture. The very first wallpaper he designed, the 'Trellis' pattern, is in the lobby. One of his most popular – 'Willow-boughs' – appears in the Willow Bedroom.

There are more examples at Wightwick Manor in the West Midlands, where rooms are named after Morris papers – the Acanthus Room and Pomegranate Passage.

Eighteenth-century Dutch tile

Minton tile (1870)

Tile Style

Tiles are practical. They are hard-wearing and easy to clean, making them ideal for bathrooms, kitchens, on walls, floors, even around fireplaces. But they can be decorative, too. The process of making patterns on tile was revolutionised in the 1750s when transfer printing was invented. Until then all patterns had to be painted by hand.

Colours and designs reflect the fashions of the time. In the eighteenth century, blue and white patterns were influenced by Chinese porcelain. The Victorians preferred images of birds, flowers, and classical myths, often in dark colours.

Copy Cats

These patterns could be for tiles, ceilings or even a book cover. They are in fact from a seventeenth-century gardening book and they are designs for knot gardens, low hedges grown in complicated shapes, which were fashionable in Tudor times. The two shown were actually used to create the knot garden at Little Moreton Hall

Print Your Own Patterns

You might not be able to make your own wallpaper, but you could print patterns on a smaller scale – perhaps sheets of wrapping paper – using the same methods employed years ago. You can do simple printing using sponges, leaves, vegetables, pieces of wood or other natural objects. Think about the sort of pattern you want – will it be symmetrical? Will you alternate different shapes or colours? Think about what kind of paper it is best to use – strong brown paper, thin tissue paper. Will you let each colour dry first or let them merge?

Home comforts

Take a Seat!

For a long time chairs were only for important people – everyone else made do with benches and stools. Yet chairs would have been no more comfortable – they were still wooden and hard. Chairs were not padded or upholstered until about the seventeenth century when people wanted more comfort in their homes – though another reason may have been the change in men's dress from well padded trousers to breeches!

From the mid 1600s onwards, cabinet-making, as it was called, got better and better. Furniture became lighter and better adapted to varying needs. Advances in technological skills meant there were new shapes and designs to suit every occasion and taste, from day beds, a form of couch with an adjustable end, upholstered armchairs – called sleeping chairs – and eventually sofas, with backs and arms.

Chairs without arms, called farthingale chairs, were introduced in the early seventeenth century specially for women who wore wide skirts, called farthingales, that were fashionable at that time.

In the late eighteenth century it was the fashion to cover settees and chairs in specially woven tapestries.

Furniture became very ornate and decorative. In the early eighteenth century or Regency period, gilded bronze – or ormolu – was popular and everything was gilt or painted gold, much like the style of Louis XIV in France. Where wood was used it was often inlaid with other decorative materials such as ebony, ivory, mother-of-pearl, marble or tortoiseshell.

By the Victorian era furniture was machine-made and the construction of chairs was hidden under layers of stuffing and covered in plush velvet with deep buttons. It was then that the Arts and Crafts designers, who rejected mass production, encouraged a return to traditional crafts, with simple styles and natural materials.

Victorian chaise-longue

Table Manners

The first tables were nothing more than wooden boards laid on trestles. The word table comes from the Latin 'tabula' meaning a board. This meant that they could be put away when they were not being used. In small houses which often only had one room this was quite an advantage. Later they became stronger with carved legs and were an important feature of a dining room, especially in large houses where guests were entertained.

The seventeenth-century oak table in the firehouse at Townend, a farmhouse in Cumbria, is so huge it had to be put together where it was to be used. The Browne family, who lived there, personalised much of their furniture by carving patterns, dates and heraldic devices on it. George Browne (1834-1914) was a gifted joiner and woodcarver and the rooms are full of ornate examples of his work.

Sofa at Kedleston Hall

Most tables for formal occasions were long, narrow and rectangular so that people could chat to the person sitting opposite and the host could sit at the head of the table, the most important position. Other tables were designed as pieces of furniture in their own right. For example, the table in the High Great Chamber at Hardwick Hall, Derbyshire, was probably made to celebrate the marriage of Bess of Hardwick to the Earl of Shrewsbury in 1568. It is decorated with a complicated inlay pattern of musical instruments, playing cards, board games and even a sheet of music.

The round table in the dressing room at Castle Drogo in Devon, was Julius Drewe's rent table, so called because the drawers round the side were for the rent payments from his tenants. It is cleverly designed to rotate so that he could reach each drawer without having to get up!

Thomas Chippendale

Thomas Chippendale (1718-79) was one of the most famous of all English furniture makers. Among the finest things he made were chairs with beautifully carved and decorated backs. His designs were copied by many other companies and in 1754 he published a book illustrating all the various styles he liked to use. It was called *The Gentleman and Cabinet-Maker's Director* and it marked a turning point for design. Publications like this suggested designers were no longer simple rural craftsmen but sophisticated businessmen. Chippendale's customers, for example, were rich and distinguished people and he designed furniture for several large country houses.

What sort of chair do you think this might be? For whom or what purpose could it possibly have been designed for? No, it's not a dentist's chair and it's not a whoopee cushion! It is in fact an exercise chair or 'chamber horse' – you bounced up and down on it to keep fit! It was made for the Viscount Tyrconnel and is on show at Belton House in Lincolnshire.

Stop Press!

Can you guess what this is? Here's a clue – it stands outside the door of the dining room at Castle Drogo. It's a napkin press designed to make sure guests always had nice crisp table linen!

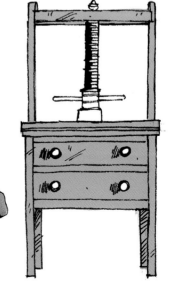

Creature Comforts!

At East Riddlesden Hall, Yorkshire, most of the furniture is locally made but some of it is unusual. There is a shepherd's chair, built with a hutch underneath it to hold a dog or a lamb.

Every part of a piece of furniture is designed – down to the feet! Which is the odd one out?

And so to beds...

Sweet Dreams

When you think that you spend about a third of your life asleep, it's hardly surprising that a bed has always been one of the most important items of furniture in any house. Years ago a good bed was expensive and, once bought or made, it often became a family heirloom to be handed down from generation to generation.

State bedchamber at Osterley

Early beds – what we call four-posters – had a wooden frame, often with posts, a roof (or tester), and a headboard. They were hung with curtains which were pulled round to keep out the draughts – there was no central heating in those days! The curtains were the most important part in terms of status symbol and were as good as the owner could afford. The higher and more elaborate the posts, and the more the curtains were adorned with tassels, fringes and embroideries, the more the owner was seen to be rich and important.

Little and Large

There is a bed made of slate at Penryhn Castle, in North Wales, which weighs more than a ton! In the nursery at Berrington Hall, in Sleaford and Worcester, there is a delightful miniature four-poster bed.

State Bed at Kedleston Hall

There are no less than three state beds at Knole in Kent. There is one in the Venetian Ambassador's Room, which was made for James II and furnished with sumptuous green velvet. The Spangle Bed is hung with crimson satin and covered with hundreds of sequins. But neither of these can compare with the King's Bed with its cloth of gold and silver, lined with salmon pink satin and embroidered with black and silver thread.

A state bed hung with embroidered Chinese silk arrived at Calke Abbey, Derbyshire, in the eighteenth century but was never unpacked from its cases. As a result the old silk has not faded or rotted with age and light. It has now been assembled and is on display behind glass to protect it. It is embroidered with dragons, birds, deer and other traditional motifs in brilliant blues, reds, greens and oranges.

Material world

Off the Wall

Today our walls are decorated – covered with either paper or paint – but in the past they were often bare stone, brick or even rubble. Because they were so cold, dull and dirty, people who lived in large houses covered them up.

The earliest wall covering was tapestry which stayed in fashion for a long time.

Another material used was leather. The walls of the dining room at Bateman's, are hung with Cordoba leather – so called, in East Sussex, because that type of leather was made centuries ago in Cordoba, Spain. It was first covered with a silver foil and then yellow varnish to look like gold. When this was dry the surface was stamped or tooled to give it depth and the design was painted on using oils.

Some of the first wallpapers came from the Far East. Early wallpapers were made in fairly small sheets and were either hand-painted or printed with carved wooden blocks. They were glued to canvas before being pasted to the wall or nailed on to wooden battens.

The Victorians liked complicated patterned wallpapers in shades of rich green and maroon for the simple practical reason that they didn't show the smoke stains caused by the open coal fires in their homes.

From Rushes to Rugs

Carpets are quite a modern invention. In medieval times, most rugs and carpets were designed to be used on furniture, as coverings for tables or chests. Rushes or straw were strewn on the floor, as well as herbs and sweet smelling flowers in summer to hide the smell of the dirt which piled up. The rushes made it easier to sweep up the dust. Later, straw was plaited into mats for the important rooms of the house, similar to that which can be seen today in the long gallery at Montacute.

In the seventeenth century, floor carpets were made of different materials – one of the most surprising used is leather – but wool was the most common, and the warmest. Imagine how much work went in to weaving them by hand. They were not machine made until the nineteenth century.

Window Dressing

It's hard to find out what fabrics looked like a very long time ago because there are none left to see. Many simply wore out from use but light, dust and even changes in temperature can do a lot of damage. That's why in some houses you'll notice that rooms are kept quite dark. We have to rely on what people wrote about textiles. Inventories are a good source of information. They are lists of the contents of a house which were made when someone died.

When the Trust bought Calke Abbey in Derbyshire, some curtains made of luxurious yellow silk tissue were found to be in poor condition. The effect of light had almost reduced them to powder. To reproduce the pattern every intersection of the warp and weft was noted on graph paper – over a million squares! – and the fabric was painstakingly restored.

In the sixteenth century, 'curtains' were the hangings round a bed – it was rare to see them at windows where wooden shutters were needed to keep out the cold and rain. As windows became more prominent features of a house, so fabrics draped around them helped to make them even more eye-catching. They also made a room feel warm and comfortable and gave privacy.

During the eighteenth century, new fabrics from the East influenced styles. Printed cottons and linens became available, especially chintz from India. These were also much easier to wash than the heavy English woollen material, which was soon tarnished by smoke from bedroom fires, so they were far more practical.

The windows and bed in the West Turret bedroom at Blickling Hall are hung with 300-year-old crewel embroideries which were discovered in the attics. Crewel work is named after the fine woollen thread called crewel which was used to work the stitches.

How does your garden grow?

The First Gardeners

The Romans were probably the first to create gardens in Britain. Their taste for style and good living demanded pleasant surroundings outside as well as inside. Ornaments such as statues and vases, as well as columns, porticoes, fountains and trellises, provided decoration. Plants were grown not to admire but to eat and to use – for making wines, dyes and perfumes and for medicinal purposes. Many gardens were courtyards within villas, surrounded by rooms on all four sides, and so had to be attractive from all angles.

From House to Horizon

By the end of the seventeenth century the English garden had merged into the surrounding park land. The main influence behind this trend was France, where the garden designer, Le Notre, had laid out the great gardens of Versailles for King Louis XIV. His gardens were designed symmetrically around a main axis, or dividing line, which stretched from the house as far as the eye could see, crossing formal beds (parterres) and circling lakes and canals. Other avenues radiated from it in all directions and between them were pavilions, fountains, triumphal arches and statues, often sited with mathematical precision. Nothing this grand was ever built in England but many of the features were copied on a smaller scale and Charles II, who spent his years of exile in France, led the way by choosing French landscape designers to remodel the gardens at Hampton Court.

Can you fill in the missing half of the garden below?

Parterre at Oxburgh Hall

Fair and Square

The Tudors gave real thought to how their gardens looked, designing them for enjoyment as well as practical use. A typical Tudor garden was square and bordered by walls or hedges. The square would be divided up by paths of gravel, sand, turf or scented herbs with square or oblong flower beds in the spaces between. Soon it became the fashion to grow low hedges of lavender or rosemary around the beds and use small plants, coloured gravel and sand to make a pattern within them. The designs for these grew so complicated they became known as knot gardens.

The Knot Garden at Little Moreton Hall

Natural Beauty

In the eighteenth century, designers turned to the natural beauty of the English countryside for inspiration, recreating parks with winding streams, green pastures and shady woods. Many of them saw nature through the eyes of famous painters, especially Claude and Poussin – French landscape painters of the seventeenth century who had painted idealised scenes of the Italian countryside. Gardens became sophisticated art forms with classical temples, ruins and bridges.

Lancelot 'Capability' Brown (1716-83), the famous landscape designer who earned his nickname because he often told clients that their gardens had 'capabilities', was the leading figure in what became known as the Landscape Movement. His materials were the contours of the land, grass, water and trees – he saw no need for temples and statues. He controlled landscapes, damming streams to build great lakes and planting clumps of trees to frame a scene. Capability Brown was criticised for destroying beautiful gardens, preferring to sweep the lawns right up to the house, but his aim was to keep things simple at a time when many designs were over-elaborate.

Humphrey Repton (1752-1818) followed in Capability Brown's footsteps, though rarely on the same scale, and was brought in to adapt some of Brown's original landscapes. The main difference was that Repton, who believed that the house must blend into the garden, reintroduced flower-beds, terraces and rose gardens near the house. His success was largely due to his businesslike approach with clients whom he gave individual attention, producing a Red Book – a portfolio of notes and before-and-after sketches bound in red leather – for every project.

Hedge your Bets

At Knightshayes Court, Devon, there is a topiary with five hounds chasing a fox sculpted out of a yew hedge. It is said that once a gardener cut a hole at the end of the hedge so that the fox could escape! Our word 'topiary' comes from the Latin word for gardener, topiarius.

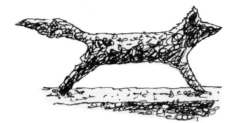

Topiary fox at Knightshayes

Flower Power

Gertrude Jekyll was a painter and craftswoman who lived at the end of the nineteenth century. When her eyesight began to fail she turned her talents to gardens, designing them as though she were composing a picture. She cleverly planned year-round colour by dividing beds up to bloom in different seasons.

Your Own Backyard

The average garden today is designed for people not plants – an outdoor room in which to sit and relax or entertain friends. On modern estates or in roads where houses all look the same, gardens give people a chance to express their own style. Even the smallest gardens can be transformed with window boxes and hanging baskets.

There are many points to consider when designing a garden – the soil, whether it is in sun or shade, flat or on a slope, but probably the most important factors are how you want to use it and how much time you can or want to spend on it. Paved patios with plants in containers save mowing grass. Ground-cover plants which spread quickly stop weeds growing.

Heaven Scent

Some gardens are designed in terms of their fragrance. These gardens are particularly important for people with impaired sight.

Ancient splendor

Made to Order

The Ancient Greeks designed some of the most beautiful buildings ever made, and many dramatic ruins remain for us to admire. The most striking feature of Classical Greek architecture was the tall elegant columns, often supporting triangular gable ends or pediments decorated with friezes. The Greeks based their designs on three different styles of column: Doric, Ionic and Corinthian. The Romans, who adapted Greek architecture, added two styles of their own: Tuscan and Composite. In early temples, these columns were made of wood and often painted in strong colours. Later they were built of limestone or marble and embellished with sculpture.

Urns and Amphoras

The ancient Greeks made beautifully decorated pottery. Their designs, based on geometric patterns as well as scenes from daily life, were painted on reddish brown clay in iron oxide. This turned black when fired, with striking results.

Greek vases were made in different shapes, each with names, according to their use – for example, the amphora with its two handles was for storing oil, water or wine. The kylix was a drinking cup. More slender shapes were for perfume and cosmetics.

The most famous example of Classical Greek architecture is the temple of the Parthenon, which stands high above the city of Athens on a hill called the Acropolis.

It is very cleverly designed. The Greeks had quite strict rules to follow to make sure their buildings were well-proportioned.

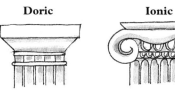

| Doric | Ionic |
| Corinthian | Composite |

Great Works of Art

Statues were an important part of classical temples and Greek sculptors, by experimenting and using their knowledge of how the body worked, perfected the art of representing the human form in a realistic way. Paintings on pottery survive to show the Greeks' skill in perspective drawing. For the first time in history artists learned to paint people face on, not just in profile, so that they were three-dimensional and life-like.

What a Performance

The Greeks built great open-air theatres hollowed out of the hillside, such as the one at Epidauros which is still used today. Tiers of stone seats were arranged in a horse-shoe shape around the circular paved area called the orchestra. It was designed with such precision that everyone in the audience could see and even people on the back row could hear everything. Many modern theatres use the same principles.

Modern sports stadia are usually round, similar to the ancient Roman amphitheatres where gladiators staged displays of combat.

Down to the Last Detail

Architectural detailing played an important part in classical design and graceful mouldings in a range of set patterns were used not only on buildings but also on pots and furniture.

The leaves of the acanthus plant, a favourite motif of Greek artists, appears at the top of Corinthian columns. It was adopted hundreds of years later by William Morris who liked to use natural images on his wallpapers and textiles.

The palmette design appears on marble friezes on buildings, on pottery and on furniture. The Greek key or fret design is an example of the popularity of geometrical patterns.

Many designers later adapted these motifs to evoke a classical mood. Among Robert Adam's favourite images, for example, were Greek urns, scrolls, rams' heads and wheat husks. He used them on his furniture as well as ceiling mouldings and mirror decorations.

Palmette

Greek Key pattern

European Highlights

In the eighteenth century, if you were the son of nobility or from a wealthy family, you would almost certainly go off on what became known as the Grand Tour, visiting the classical sites of Ancient Greece and Rome, often with a tutor. The tour became an essential part of the education of most young noblemen and they experienced at first hand the culture they had learned so much about from great works of literature. On their return, many wanted suitable houses in which to display the collections of paintings and classical sculptures they had bought.

Wheat husk

Urn

Underneath the Arches

The Romans adopted many Greek styles for their own purposes but something that they developed themselves was the arch, a great feat of engineering which enabled them to build incredible bridges and aqueducts throughout their empire as well as bold triumphal arches dedicated to mighty gods and emperors.

Their ability to build arches also helped them to make vaulted roofs, such as the Pantheon in Rome, a huge domed hall with a circular opening at the top to let in light. Such designs were built with a kind of concrete made from pieces of broken stone or brick mixed into a mortar of lime and sand.

At Kedleston Hall, Derbyshire, Adam created a monumental marble hall with ten alabaster columns rising like tree trunks on either side and classical statues along the walls. It is lit from above like the open courtyard of a Roman villa.

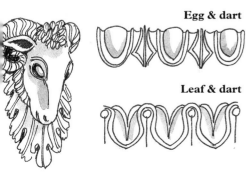

Egg & dart

Leaf & dart

19

Under the influence

It's All Greek to Me

Throughout history, generations of designers have tried to imitate the skills and artistry of the Ancient Greeks and Romans.

In the late 1700s, some architects had draughtsmen picture their buildings in ruins before they were even built so that they could compare them with the noble ruins of the ancient world!

Today the classical Greek style is a familiar sight in many towns in this country. That is because in the eighteenth century, the great architecture of Greek temples was adapted to churches, palaces and many public buildings such as town halls, courts, banks, museums and libraries.

The style was used to make important buildings seem grand and serious because of its links with a great civilisation.

Eventually, elements began to appear in houses as well. One of the first houses in England to have a grand classical entrance – called a portico – was The Vyne in Hampshire.

But how could architects have known what ancient buildings looked like inside when all that was left for them to model their ideas on were ruins? Their answer was to use the same features inside, such as columns and colonnades, as they did outside.

Others followed the fashions of the time, resulting in the strange combination of formal exteriors with lavish interiors, such as Berrington Hall in Hereford and Worcester.

The new enthusiasm for classical architecture coincided with new archaeological finds. Between 1751-55 James Stuart and Nicholas Revett prepared the first measured drawings ever made of these then little-known buildings, and published the first volume of their *Antiquities of Athens* in 1762. The Society of Dilettanti, founded in 1733-34 by a group of rich young noblemen, aimed to promote 'Greek taste and Roman spirit' and acted as patrons of designers and architects by financing archaeologists and scholars.

Building on the Past

Robert Adam spent three years in Italy studying Roman architecture. He was so impressed by what he saw that when he came back to England he developed a distinctive neo-classical style and was invited by the owners of many country estates to give their homes a classical 'face-lift'.

The Etruscan Dressing Room at Osterley is one of Adam's masterpieces. The room was inspired by Etruscan vases found at Pompeii and uses the same terracotta red and black colour scheme to portray typical Greek motifs. The door panels, the cane-seated chairs and the canvas chimney board are all painted to match the walls. Most visitors to Osterley in the eighteenth century would have recognised these images.

The Portico (The Vyne)

Pillers and Porticoes

William Anson was responsible for building Shugborough in Staffordshire, but it was his eldest son who turned it into a fine park and important country seat. Thomas Anson was a great admirer of the arts of classical Greece and a founder member of the Society of Dilettanti. He filled the house with classical statues and marble busts, and hung paintings of classical ruins in the dining room.

When Thomas' great-nephew inherited Shugborough he chose the architect Samuel Wyatt, a leading neo-classical designer, to help him with the alterations. He completely changed its proportions by building a vast eight-columned portico across the front of the house. Inside, Doric columns were introduced into the hall to create an appropriate setting for the fine Greek and Roman sculpture collected by Thomas Anson.

Classical Cabinet

This is not a wooden model of a classical house but a cigar cabinet with columns and pediment! It sits in Mr Drewe's dressing room at Castle Drogo, Devon.

Pot Black

One of the most famous English potters was inspired by the ceramic art of the past. Josiah Wedgwood (1730-95) was a shrewd businessman who anticipated the vogue for the neo-classical style. He was also interested in inventing new materials and methods and his great ambition was to make decorative vases to compare with those of the ancient Greeks.

Classical Bust

Temples of Delight

In the grounds at Stowe in Buckinghamshire you can wander through the Elysian Fields or along the Grecian Valley. There is a Palladian bridge, a Corinthian Arch, and everywhere you go you come across temples – 32 to be precise! There were once as many as 50!

Funnily enough Stowe was owned by the Temple family whose motto was Templa Quam Dilecta – how delightful are thy temples!

Palladian Bridge at Stowe

Some of his first productions were enormous vases with copies of Greek paintings in matt-surfaced red and white enamels on a black background – the only difference was that he clothed the nude bodies to suit delicate English tastes! He spent several years trying to come up with an accurate reproduction of a Roman work in coloured glass – the famous Barberini or Portland Vase of which less than 50 copies were made.

Eastern promise

A Taste of the Exotic

Today we can learn about other countries from books and television. Modern travel makes it easy to visit them. But years ago, when explorers were only just beginning to discover that distant countries even existed, people were naturally fascinated by these exotic far-away lands.

The East, in particular, was seen as a fabulous, fairy-tale place. When the East India Company, founded in 1601, began trading with India, China and Japan, and importing light cottons, luxurious silks, delicate white porcelain and wallpaper, the fashion for the Chinese style really took off. It was known as Chinoiserie.

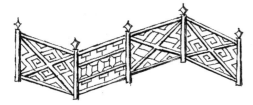

The Lacquered Look

The craft of lacquering furniture was popular in China and Japan where they used the sap from the lac tree as a protective and decorative varnish. Examples of imported lacquer work were highly prized and European craftsmen began by trying to make copies using varnish instead of lacquer. It was called 'japanned' furniture. However, they soon began to add their own touches and introduce European figures into their designs along with exotic animals such as monkeys and arabesque or scrollwork patterns, as well as using bright colours such as scarlet, yellow, blue and green, instead of the conventional black and gold.

Vase from Belton House

Pots and Plates

Porcelain was unknown in Britain until it was imported from China. People were used to brown clay pots and earthenware dishes and were fascinated by the beauty of porcelain which is pure white. Many potters tried to discover how it was made. In France they managed to make a kind of porcelain called soft-paste. It became known as Sévres after the place near Paris where the factory was built. German potters at the Meissen factory developed a hard paste. English potters were finally successful when kaolin or china clay deposits, needed to make porcelain, were found in Cornwall. Only then could they copy the blue and white designs made popular by Chinese porcelain.

Fine Fabrics

English merchants traded woollen cloths for lighter fabrics such as pretty Indian prints and silks. People preferred them to the old tapestry curtains and hangings which were dull, heavy and difficult to wash. The problem was that people stopped buying English cloth and put English weavers out of work. In 1696 an Act was passed making it illegal to wear anything printed in China, and in 1720 fines were introduced for using Chinese material on beds, chairs or cushions! So English designers tried to imitate the Chinese look, making fabrics printed with little bridges, pagodas or Chinese temples and figures carrying sunshades.

The most famous porcelain design is the Willow Pattern, with its weeping willow, pagoda building, three people on a bridge and the pair of swallows. The legend behind the scene which tells how two lovers were turned into the swallows is English and not Chinese!

Oriental Gardens

The scene from a Willow Pattern plate is brought to life at Biddulph Grange Garden in Staffordshire. In a corner of the garden, called China, there is an ornate wooden bridge over a pool, a Chinese temple, a dragon parterre cut out of the turf and even part of the Great Wall! This elaborate setting was created by the imaginative nineteenth-century botanist, James Bateman, to display exotic plants that were being brought back from the Far East.

Chinese Rooms

In the eighteenth century, any country house whose owner wanted to keep up with the latest fashions had to have a Chinese Room. The main feature was often the painted wallpaper. Chinese papers – often called 'India papers' because they were brought to England by the East India Company – set the trend for wallpaper generally.

The state bedchamber at Nostell Priory, in Yorkshire, has 18 sheets of Chinese paper depicting every sort of bird in brilliant blues, pinks and greens. There is Chippendale furniture to match, with green and gold lacquer and chinoiserie patterns.

The Chinese bedroom at Belton House, Lincolnshire, is hung with a well-preserved eighteenth-century wallpaper, decorated with a continuous scene of a garden party running around the lower part. The bed is painted to look like bamboo.

Ducks, silver pheasants and birds of paradise fly among lotus flowers and peonies on the walls in the Chinese bedroom at Felbrigg Hall, Norfolk.

The world's greatest example of chinoiserie is the Royal Pavilion, Brighton, with its great onion-shaped domes. It was built for the Prince Regent, at the beginning of the nineteenth century. He was infatuated with the oriental style. Inside the walls are draped with yellow fabric to look like Chinese tents and bells and tassels hang from the ceilings.

Up in arms!

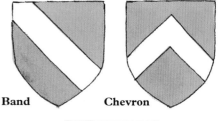

Band **Chevron**

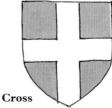

Cross

Who's Who?

Coats of arms were first designed to be used on shields in battle so that soldiers could tell who was on their side – with full face helmets and suits of armour it was quite difficult to tell who was who!

The objects on the shield had to be simple and bold in design so that they could be seen clearly. The earliest coats of arms often contained nothing more than a coloured bar, a cross or an animal.

Window at Speke Hall

Jousting tournaments were a chance for knights to show off their family crests. They were embroidered on their horses' saddle-cloths and on banners as well as the knights' tunics or surcoats – which is where we get the name, 'coat of arms'.

Ever since the Middle Ages craftsmen have used heraldry as a subject for wood and stone carving and stained glass. Gradually, designs were used in the decoration of the family estate rather than on the battlefield and were a way of displaying a family's importance. Many castles and great houses have heraldic ceilings, fireplaces and windows and coats of arms above their entrance gates or porches and in other prominent places.

The wooden panels lining the walls of the winter parlour at Canons Ashby, Northamptonshire, are decorated with brightly coloured crests. They commemorate the ancestry of Sir Erasmus Dryden who inherited the house in 1584, though some are there for fun and for visitors to work out their meaning.

The fireplace at Calke Abbey

A Family Affair

In the Middle Ages, every noble family had their own personal emblem. Kings and princes sometimes granted them to their subjects but usually people invented them for themselves. However, as more and more people did this there was a danger of designs being duplicated and there were in fact many disagreements. In 1484 the College of Arms was founded to ensure that no two families carried the same coat of arms. As a result, the designs on shields became more and more complicated to avoid confusion.

Coats of Many Colours

Heraldry became an important and established system all over Europe and there was a strict set of rules for the designs and colours which could be used. The colours are divided into:

The metals	The tinctures	
r = gold	gules	= red
rgent = silver (or white)	vert	= green
	sable	= black
	azure	= blue
	purpure	= purple

Two patterns representing fur can also be used. These are called ermine and vair.

The names for these colours – and many other parts of heraldry – are based on medieval French, which was spoken in the English court at the time.

The Lion and the Unicorn

Animals were favourite symbols on shields. The lion is the most common and often appears in a position known as rampant – upright with its front paws raised.

At Castle Drogo, in Devon, the Drewe lion keeps guard over the entrance and appears in several rooms. The architect Lutyens made it a design feature of the latch on the door leading into the library.

Other popular wild animals included boars, elephants, leopards, bears and wolves.

Stars and Stripes

Everything that is put on a shield is called a charge. Here are some examples:

The objects on the shield often have a meaning connected with the person who uses them. Some people had fun by making puns on words. For example, the Lucy family of Charlecote used three pike on their shield as the heraldic term for these fish was 'lucie'. Perhaps you can think of a pun for your name.

Hunting was one of the main sports in the Middle Ages, so dogs often appear on shields, especially the foxhound and the greyhound. Richard Brownlow of Belton House, Lincolnshire, was granted the use of the greyhound on his crest by Queen Elizabeth I in 1593. It appears all over the house from the painted floor in the Tyrconnel Room, on the wrought iron gate, etched into door locks and even on a plate.

From Pubs to Packaging

Soldiers no longer carry shields but coats of arms and emblems are still popular. Many organisations and companies find it useful to have an emblem by which people recognise them. Crests or shields are common among banks and building societies, for example. Many pub names have links with heraldry – such as The King's Arms or, The Fleur-de-Lys.

The company logo is perhaps the modern equivalent of a coat of arms. It is usually a simple design or picture which people remember because of its visual impact and because it reminds them of the company or society it represents. The National Trust have adopted the symbol of the oak leaf. See if you can find it somewhere on this book.

Logos are also designed to present a certain image. Image is all-important in the commercial world where different companies compete to sell their products and designers are challenged to come up with ever more striking packaging and advertisements.

25

Back to basics?

New Materials, New Methods

Steel, concrete and glass have been the basic ingredients of twentieth–century design. Different tools and equipment are available today compared with 100 years ago and the skills of crafts men and women have been replaced to a great extent by machines and factory mass production. The use of cast iron had been perfected as early as 1851 when Joseph Paxton's great Crystal Palace was built in London.

By the 1880s new smelting techniques meant that steel frames could be easily made. The development of metal window frames and the ability to produce large sheets of glass made it possible to create buildings almost entirely from glass. But it was the development of reinforced concrete – concrete made even stronger by a framework of steel – which had the greatest impact, allowing architects to design bigger and higher buildings. The first skyscrapers appeared in America during the 1890s. New York's Empire State Building, built between 1929 and 1931, was an amazing 102 storeys high and for many years it was the tallest building in the world.

Plastic has revolutionised everyday objects around the home, from light switches to furniture. It is hard wearing, cheap to produce, does not rust or rot and can be moulded into any shape.

Metal supports replaced legs as early as 1929 in Mies van der Rohe's famous Barcelona chair.

Villa Savoye

The Search for a Style

This century has produced a whole variety of design styles but the main trend has been towards simplicity. The 'Modernist' or 'International' style developed out of a belief that 'form follows function' – in other words, you should be able to tell what a building is used for from its design.

The Swiss-born architect, Le Corbusier (1887-1965), was a famous Modernist who thought that houses should be designed as 'machines for living in'. He designed them according to a set plan which he called the Five Points of a New Architecture. Among these were the ideas that a building should be raised off the ground on stilts or pilotis, and that it should be open plan inside with thin horizontal windows and a flat roof. His Villa Savoye near Paris is a typical example.

A house in Hampstead stands as a lasting reminder of the ideals of Modernism. Number 2 Willow Road was built in 1938 for Ernö Goldfinger, a leading architect of the Modern Movement, who designed the house and most of the furniture and fittings as well. Inside, decoration is kept to the bare essentials. Rooms are open plan and painted strong primary colours to make them seem bigger. The house is still filled with the furniture designed for it by Goldfinger and the contemporary paintings and sculptures he and his wife collected specially to suit the style of their unique home. At the time its design caused an outcry in the neighbourhood. Today the house is listed as a building of historic interest, and is one of the most recent National Trust acquisitions.

Daring to be Different

In the last 20 years, buildings have become increasingly high-tech, with the working parts of a building – the services such as ventilation ducts, plumbing and heating pipes and even escalators and lifts – appearing on the outside. This makes maintenance easier as well as creating a certain visual effect or image. Colour is often used for practical purposes. On the Pompidou Centre in Paris, designed by Richard Rogers and Reizo Piano in 1969, the services are colour-coded – green is for water, blue for the air-conditioning and yellow for electricity. Richard Rogers' company used the same approach on the controversial Lloyd's Building in London.

Turning Green

Today we are all more aware of the harm people can do to the environment. The result is that design is influenced by the realisation that many natural resources or materials are being used up too quickly. Buildings are now given insulated walls and double-glazing to save energy. Timber is grown specially, to save felling trees in the rain forests, and different materials are being tried out. For example, a new National Trust Visitor's Centre at Langdon Cliffs, on the White Cliffs of Dover, has a grass roof. Not only does turf provide good insulation but it is a plentiful and cheap resource which also allows the building to blend into its surroundings.

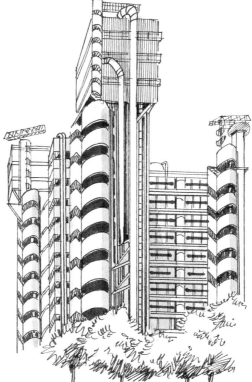

Lloyd's Building, London

Learning by Mistakes

When whole cities were flattened by bombs during the Second World War it led to a serious shortage of houses. Tower blocks seemed like the ideal solution, but although they worked in theory, in practice the people who lived in them felt isolated and their quality of life was poor. High-rise blocks are now being demolished in favour of low-rise housing schemes with gardens and local landmarks and amenities such as pubs, churches and shops are retained.

**Fountains Abbey
Visitor Centre**

As more houses were built more furniture was needed and during the Second World War something called 'utility furniture' was mass produced as a stop-gap. It soon got a reputation for being shoddy and poor quality. The problem was that designers did not know how to design furniture to be made by machines. They had to learn how to use machines to do the work for which they were best suited. A design committee was set up by the government to suggest improvements. One of the points that it made was that furniture must look good as well as being functional and be designed for the age in which it is made.

Boosbeck Industries was based at Ormesby Hall, in Cleveland, and made plain, high-quality furniture by hand, to order, in the 1930s and 40s.

Bridging the Gap

Many designers are now rediscovering the value of traditional materials such as bricks, stone and wood but using them in a new way. The new Visitors' Centre at Fountains Abbey in Yorkshire is arranged around a courtyard to look like a group of farm buildings, and its tiles and dry stone walling blend in with the local landscape. The sweeping s-shaped roof is covered in stone slates and lead, and the timber structure of the roof can be seen inside, along with the steel frame which is also exposed in places outside. It is a building which bridges the gap between traditional and modern in a new and exciting way.

Weird and wonderful designs

Shell Shock

Shells have been used as decorative motifs for centuries but the fashion really took off in England in the 1600s when the fourth Duke of Bedford built a shell grotto at Woburn Abbey, now the oldest surviving example of shell work in the country. Shell work soon became a popular hobby for well-to-do ladies who covered garden pots, mirrors and trinket boxes. Jane and Mary Parminter, spinster cousins, lived in an unusual 16-sided folly called A La Ronde, near Exmouth in Devon. Everywhere you turn there are shells, from the fireplace to the staircase, but their masterpiece is the Shell Gallery, a mass of shells in swirls and zig-zags which took them eleven years and boxloads of shells to create.

Can you design your own shell collage or picture? Draw the outline on some thick card first.

Shell architecture became something of a speciality in the eighteenth century. Sea captains brought back shells from their travels to new-found shores and many towns near a beach had a small shell house.

Leith Hill Tower

Sheer Folly

The great monuments of Ancient Greece and Rome were admired not only as fine architecture but as romantic ruins, and in the late eighteenth century, picturesque ruined towers and castles were built in the grounds of many country houses.

Mow Cop in Cheshire looks like a ruined castle perched high on its hill. It is actually a summerhouse, built for the local landowner, Randle Wilbraham, in 1754.

Some follies are even more sinister and mysterious because they are tombs or burial monuments. Leith Hill Tower in Surrey stands on top of the highest point of south-east England. It was built in

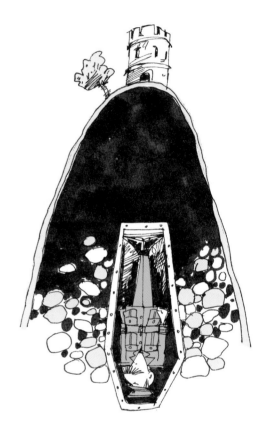

1766 by Richard Hull who is buried on the spot. On the top of Box Hill, Surrey, sits a round tower said to stand over the grave of Major Peter Labelliere who was buried 100 feet down and head first because he believed that at the Resurrection the world would be turned topsy-turvy and he would be the only one left standing on his feet!

Many are sited on hilltops with magnificent views. The Pepperbox in Wiltshire, for example, may have been intended as a viewpoint from which ladies could follow the hunt in comfort. This red brick octagonal three-storey tower, complete with weathervane, was built in 1606 and may be the earliest folly in England.

Grotty Grottoes!

Why would anyone want a dark, damp cave at the bottom of the garden? People wanted just that in the eighteenth century – they saw them as quiet peaceful places, somewhere to rest in the cool and shade. They were either mossy and dark or lined with shells, mirror glass or stones. Greenery and ferns thrived amid the dripping water. At Stourhead in Wiltshire a Nymph of the Grotto lies amongst the stones and stalactites!

All Creatures Great and Small

Rococo, an ornate yet elegant style of decoration popular in the eighteenth century, gave rise to some weird and wonderful features, often inspired by the natural and supernatural world. Claydon House in Buckinghamshire is full of extraordinary carvings by the eccentric craftsman Luke Lightfoot. He transformed wood into wonderful birds and strange creatures called wyverns – winged, two-legged scaly monsters, with wings outstretched and claws bared.

Pietro Lanfrancini's magnificent plasterwork in the saloon at Wallington, Northumberland, features winged sphinxes perched on curling foliage, garlands of flowers and cornucopias – horns – overflowing with fruit.

Watch for the Birdies!

Wherever you look in Clandon Park, Surrey, there are birds – in paintings, carved in wood on the staircase, decorating tables and mantelpieces, and as the brackets for wall lights. The rare collection of porcelain birds from China was collected by Mrs David Gubbay who spent her childhood in India surrounded by exotic birds. A spectacular phoenix presides over the state bedroom.

Ceiling is Believing!

Have you ever heard of a ceiling with legs? If you look up in the marble hall at Clandon Park you will see an amazing three-dimensional plaster ceiling. Larger than life figures, their legs hanging over the edge of the cornice, look as if they could leap down at any minute!

Tea and Sympathy

A bizarre Meissen tea set in the parlour at Wallington has paintings of life-size insects nestling in the bottom of each cup. Maybe they were they designed to frighten off unwelcome guests!

Stone Faced

The architect of Penrhyn, Thomas Hopper, had a vivid imagination. Inside, incredible carvings of strange heads peer down from the top of the stone pillars.

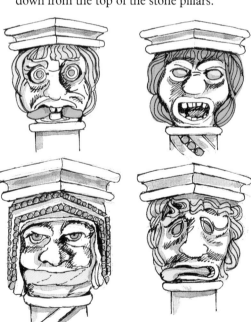

Designed for Dolls

The collection of dolls' houses in the Servants' Hall at Wallington date from 1835-1930 and range from the enormous Hammond House which is over 8 feet tall to the Mouse House which can only be seen through two keyholes and a mouse hole!

100 BC
Chinese invent paper

Furniture is mainly oak
beech, ash & elm

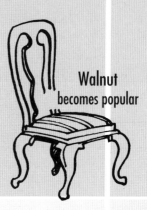

Walnut
becomes popular

1660
Mirror glass is

THE Design Timelin

454 BC The Parthenon
Athens, complete

Chinese porcelain
arrives in the West

Tudors
create knot gardens

East India Company founded;
Eastern influences begin to appear

120 AD The Pantheon
Rome, built

Tattershall Castle
Early example of brick, **1430**

Tudor houses
built with timber frames

The Great Fire
wood used less in h

THE NATIONAL TRUST

Investigating Design

Barrow

Design for Grecian Chair

porcelain made in
ope at Meissen

1865, First plastic invented
(celluloid)

Ormolu - gilded bronze
- popular in interiors and on furniture

Reinforced concrete
developed

imported from USA
ought iron appears

1825, First machine - made bricks

1909, Plastic
called Bakelite invented

1745, Porcelain factories
founded in England

Plate glass invented

Methods of iron smelting developed

1856, Bessener Process
of making steel
in bulk invented

Mass production
developed

1769, Wedgwood's Etruria
a factory built with
all processes on same site

Furniture machine-made

New interest in
traditional crafts

landscaped

Victorian terraces
built in overcrowded towns

First power station
1880, built to provide
electricity for private homes

The Pompidou Centre
1977, Paris

First iron bridge
1781, Shropshire

The Great Exhibition
1851, Crystal Palace -
first metal construction in building

First skyscrapers
1880's built in USA

Most homes
have electricity, 1930s

Brighton Pavilion
built in 1815

Public Health Act
1875, sewers, drains
water supply

Le Corbusier's
Villa Savoye built

High-tech
Buildings

Humphrey Repton
(1752 -1818)

Josiah Wedgwood
(1730 -1895)

Robert Adam
(1728 -1792)

Chippendale (1718 -1779)

Brown (1716 -1783)

William Morris
(1834 -1896)

Philip Webb
(1831 -1915)

Arts & Crafts Movement

Gertrude Jekyll
(1843-1932)

Le Corbusier
(1887-1965)

Richard Rogers

Ernö Goldfinger

Notes for parents/teachers

Design, in its many aspects, forms part of the National Curriculum for Art, History and Technology. It is a fascinating topic which helps children to draw on their knowledge of other subjects. This book challenges children to think about how and why things are made, to learn about the materials with which they are made, and to appreciate the needs of people today and in the past. They will read, too, of the people who made them, famous designers such as Robert Adam, Capability Brown, Josiah Wedgwood and William Morris, as well as the people for whom they designed.

This book makes learning fun. It provides information in a way that is both entertaining and educational but, more importantly, it encourages children to develop a natural curiosity in the things around them and the world in which they live.

National Trust properties provide a wealth of visual resources relating to an investigation into design. Whether you visit them on a school trip or on a family day out, children will enjoy spotting unusual or clever designs and guessing why and when they were designed. Encourage them to keep a sketchpad or notebook to jot down things they see. The list of properties on this page are worth a special visit.

First published in 1995 by National Trust (Enterprises) Ltd, 36 Queen Anne's Gate, London SW1H 9AS

Registered Charity No. 205846

Copyright © The National Trust 1995

All rights reserved. No part of this publication may be reproduced, stored in a retrieval system, or transmitted by any means, electronic, mechanical, photocopying or otherwise, without prior permission of the publisher.

ISBN: 0 7078 0191 5

Designed by Blade Communications, Leamington Spa

Printed by Wing King Tong Ltd., Hong Kong

National Trust Properties of Interest

Roman
Chedworth Roman Villa

Medieval
Bodiam Castle, East Sussex
Lytes Carey Manor, Somerset
Oxburgh Hall, Norfolk
Rufford Old Hall, Lancs
Tattershall Castle, Lincolnshire

Tudor
Hardwick Hall, Derbyshire
Knole, Kent
Montacute, Somerset
The Vyne, Hampshire

Stuart
Blickling Hall, Norfolk
Corfe Castle, Dorset
Chirk Castle, North Wales
Sudbury Hall, Derbyshire

Eighteenth century (Robert Adam interiors)
Kedleston Hall, Derbyshire
Hatchlands Park, Surrey
Osterley, Middlesex
Saltram, Devon

Nineteenth century
Cragside, Northumberland
Waddesdon Manor, Bucks
Wightwick Manor, West Midlands

Twentieth century
2 Willow Rd, Hampstead
Mr Straw's House, Notts

Houses linked to the Arts & Crafts movement
Buscot, Oxfordshire
Cragside, Northumberland
Standen, Sussex
Wallington, Northumberland
Wightwick Manor, West Midlands

Fine furniture
Antony, Cornwall
Attingham Park, Shropshire
Blickling, Norfolk
Basildon Park, Berkshire
Claydon, Bucks
Dunham Massey, Cheshire
Erddig, North Wales
Nostell Priory, Yorkshire
Packwood House Warwickshire
Petworth House, Sussex
Saltram, Devon
Wallington, Northumberland

Tapestries
Anglesey Abbey, Cambs
Blickling Hall, Norfolk
Hardwick Hall, Derbyshire
Montacute, Somerset

Half Timbered Houses
Little Moreton Hall, Cheshire
Lower Brockhampton, Hereford & Worcester
Speke Hall, Merseyside
Rufford Old Hall, Lancashire

Chinoiserie
Beningbrough, Yorkshire
Erddig, North Wales
Fenton House, London
Shugborough, Staffordshire

Outstanding landscape gardens
Stowe, Bucks
Stourhead, Wiltshire

Gardens designed by Capability Brown
Berrington Hall, Hereford & Worcester
Charlecote Park, Warwickshire

Topiary
Ascott, Bucks
Bodnant, Clwyd
Nymans Garden, West Sussex
Packwood House, Warwickshire

Herb gardens
Acorn Bank Garden, Cumbria
Bateman's, East Sussex
Buckland Abbey, Devon
Moseley Old Hall, Staffordshire
Springhill, Co. Londonderry

Answers to Wordsearch on page 5:

brick	wood	earth
stone	iron	slate
glass	concrete	straw